I0441255

Self Publishing
vs.
Traditional Publishing

including
Ebook
Print on Demand (POD)
Vanity/Subsidy
and Amazon Options

by LeeAnne Krusemark

Self Publishing
vs.
Traditional Publishing
including
Ebook
Print on Demand (POD)
Vanity/Subsidy
and Amazon Options
by LeeAnne Krusemark

ISBN-13: 978-1515350088
ISBN-10: 1515350088

CONTENTS
Publishing Definitions
Traditional Publishing Resources
Self-Publishing Resources
50 Print-On-Demand & E-Book
Publishing Rated Resources
Amazon Options

This is intended as a reference guide to assist you in making an informed publishing decision. We provide the information; you provide the decision! And, while extensive research was done to ensure the accuracy of all the information, we cannot guarantee the validity. Please make sure you carefully review any contracts BEFORE you sign...and read the fine print!

Until recently, there were only three ways to publish your book:

1. **Submit your manuscript to Traditional Commercial Publishers**
2. **Pay a Vanity/Subsidy publisher to print 1,000 books, costing thousands**
3. **Self Publish and handle all the aspects of the process yourself**

Now there are two new forms of publishing:

1. **Print-On-Demand Publishing**
2. **E-book Publishing**

Definitions

- **A Traditional Commercial Publisher** purchases the right to publish under its own imprint and pays you a royalty on sales. They are highly selective and handle every aspect of editing, publication, distribution, and marketing. The author is not expected to pay any of these costs. The books remain in the publisher's possession until sold, and the rights are retained by the publisher until the book goes out of print.
- **A Vanity/Subsidy Publisher** prints the book at the author's expense. Costs include the publishers profit and overhead, so vanity publishing is usually more expensive than other methods of self-publishing. The author usually

gives up rights to the book while under contract. Vanity publishers do not screen for quality, and provide no editing, warehousing, or marketing services. The author must purchase a large number of books upfront (usually more than they can sell).

- **Authentic Self Publishing** requires the author to pay for the cost of publication, as well as handle all the marketing, distribution, and storage. However, because the author can put every aspect of the process out to bid rather than accepting a pre-set package of services, self publishing can be more cost-effective than vanity publishing if the author prints a large amount of books at once. All rights and proceeds belong to the author.

- **Print-On-Demand (POD) Publishing** is a combination of vanity and self publishing; the author incurs all the costs, but does not have to publish a certain amount of books. The author receives royalties for books sold by the publisher and can buy them at a reduced rate to sell personally. The author pays an upfront fee for set up and printing (and can also pay for additional services such as editing, etc.), but then decides how many books to print and pays for only those. When more are needed, they can be printed, but it usually takes a little time to deliver. The POD publisher sometimes retains rights for a certain period of time.

- **E-Book Publishing** is Internet based and is usually only successful if the author is able to drive people to a website to pay for a download of the e-book. This usually costs next to nothing to produce, but if you can't get people to buy your e-book, what's the point? If, however, you have a successful marketing plan, your profit margin is high. The e-book publisher sometimes retains rights for a certain period of time.

Traditional Commercial Publishing

With a traditional commercial publisher, make sure you have an agent who will secure the best deal for you. The more money you get, the more money they get, so they'll work as hard as they can for you. With a traditional publisher, your royalty is usually a small percentage (5-10%), compared to profit from self publishing options (10-70%), but traditional publishers can usually sell many more books than you can. Certain types of books are also not usually successful, unless published by a traditional publisher, such as children's books and mainstream fiction. The two major players in the resource market for traditional publishers are:

The Writer's Market at www.writersmarket.com
Literary Marketplace at www.literarymarketplace.com

Authentic Self Publishing
(Offset or Digital Printing)

The following printers are available nationwide for your self publishing project. Make it a point to also research printers in your area. Always remember to ask about shipping fees for the books once printed. To quickly assist you in determining if this is something you want to pursue, take a look at the basic pricing structure for printing your book. This does not take into account possible set up or shipping fees, but it gives you a starting point. This pricing is for a 300 page 5.5x8.5" paperback book (100,000 words) with a single color cover.

Quantity	100	1000	10,000
Price/Book	$10.00	$7.00	$1.00

Adibooks
Lowell, MA
adibooks.com

Alexander's Print
Lindon, UT
alexanders.com

B&B Printing
Richmond, VA
bbprintnet.com

BookMasters
Mansfield, OH
bookmasters.com

BooksjustBooks
New York, NY
booksjustbooks.com

Brenner Printing
San Antonio, TX
brennerprinting.com

Central Plains Book
Winfield, KS
centralplainsbook.com

Color House Graphics
Grand Rapids, MI
colorhousegraphics.com

DeHart's Media Services
Santa Clara, CA
deharts.com

Morgan Printing
Grafton, ND
morganprinting.com

Starnet Media
Allendale, NJ
gsgs.com

Whitehall Printing
Naples, FL
whitehallprinting.com

Print-On-Demand (POD) and E-book Publishers

More than 50 POD and E-book publishers and the fees they charge are listed, along with the royalties they pay. Understand that the lowest fees or the highest royalties may not mean the best publishing option for you. The ratings 1 (lowest) to 10 (highest) are based on fees, royalties, contract, promotion, rights, and the quality of books. Most offer both POD and E-book options. Ebook prices are typically listed at half price of the same print on demand book.

Action Tales
POD Fee: $297
POD Royalty: 50% of retail
E-book Fee: Included
E-book Royalty: 50% of retail
actiontales.com
Rating: 1 (retain rights for 2 years after contract terminated)

Apogee
POD Fee: $0
POD Royalty: 70% of retail
E-book Fee: $0
E-book Royalty: 70% of retail
apogeepublishing.com
Rating: 8 (good contract, but add-on fees exist)

Atlantic Bridge
POD Fee: $0
POD Royalty: 30% of net
E-book Fee: $0
E-book Royalty: 45% of retail
atlanticbridge.net
Rating: 9 (offers many free services)

Author House
POD Fee: $700
POD Royalty: 25% of retail
E-book Fee: $100
E-book Royalty: 25% of retail
authorhouse.com
Rating: 4 (high set up fees and add-ons are overpriced)

Aventine
POD Fee: $350
POD Royalty: 80% of net
E-book Fee: N/A
E-book Royalty: N/A
aventinepress.com
Rating: 7 (good royalty, but consider net fees)

Awe Struck
POD Fee: N/A
POD Royalty: N/A
E-book Fee: $0
E-book Royalty: 35-40% of net
awe-struck.net
Rating: 8 (good contract, but consider net fees)

Booklocker
POD Fee: $200
POD Royalty: 15-35% of retail
E-book Fee: Included
E-book Royalty: 50-70% of retail
booklocker.com
Rating: 9 (almost as good as it gets, depending on royalty)

Books for a Buck
POD Fee: N/A
POD Royalty: N/A
E-book Fee: $0
E-book Royalty: 50% of retail
booksforabuck.com
Rating: 5 (every book sells
 for only $1!)

Books Unbound
POD Fee: N/A
POD Royalty: N/A
E-book Fee: $0
E-book Royalty: 35% of retail
booksunbound.com
Rating: 8 (low royalties)

BookSurge
POD Fee: $500
POD Royalty: 25-70% of retail
E-book Fee: Included
E-book Royalty: 70% of retail
booksurgepublishing.com
Rating: 8 (good contract, but upfront fees high)

Cold Tree Press
POD Fee: $900
POD Royalty: 15-30% of retail
E-book Fee: N/A
E-book Royalty: N/A
coldtreepress.com
Rating: 4 (upfront fees high and low royalty)

Cyber Pulp
POD Fee: N/A
POD Royalty: N/A
E-book Fee: $0
E-book Royalty: 50% of net
cyberpulp.com
Rating: 5 (they offer no website to sell your books)

Cyberman Books
POD Fee: N/A
POD Royalty: N/A
E-book Fee: $0
E-book Royalty: 40% of retail
cybermanbooks.com
Rating: 2 (must give up rights for three years)

Damn Yankee
POD Fee: N/A
POD Royalty: N/A
E-book Fee: $0
E-book Royalty: 40% of retail
damnyankee.com
Rating: 6 (decent contract, but offers no marketing assistance)

Diskus
POD Fee: N/A
POD Royalty: N/A
E-book Fee: $0
E-book Royalty: 40% of retail
diskuspublishing.com
Rating: 4 (authors must buy books at full price)

Ebookomatic
POD Fee: N/A
POD Royalty: N/A
E-book Fee: $150
E-book Royalty: 50% of retail
ebookomatic.com
Rating: 5 (all add-ons have fees)

E-books on the Net
POD Fee: N/A
POD Royalty: N/A
E-book Fee: $0
E-book Royalty: 40% of retail
ebooksonthenet.com
Rating: 9 (decent royalty and good contract)

Ebookstand
POD Fee: $450-850
POD Royalty: 30% of retail
E-book Fee: Included
E-book Royalty: 50% of retail
ebookstand.com
Rating: 5 (publishing fees are high)

Echelon Press
POD Fee: $0
POD Royalty: 10% of retail
E-book Fee: Included
E-book Royalty: 50% of retail
echelonpress.com
Rating: 8 (royalties are low, but mirrors a traditional publisher)

Ellora's Cave
POD Fee: N/A
POD Royalty: N/A
E-book Fee: $0
E-book Royalty: 35% of retail
ellorascave.com
Rating: 4 (they retain rights for three years)

FabJob
POD Fee: $0
POD Royalty: 25% of retail
E-book Fee: Included
E-book Royalty: 25% of retail
fabjob.com
Rating: 8 (good marketing via their website)

Fusion Press
POD Fee: $800-$1200
POD Royalty: 40% of net
E-book Fee: N/A
E-book Royalty: N/A
authorlink.com
Rating: 4 (initial fees very high)

Gatto
POD Fee: N/A
POD Royalty: N/A
E-book Fee: $0
E-book Royalty: 40% of retail
gattopublishing.com
Rating: 8 (good royalty and only one year contract)

Golden Pillar
POD Fee: $500-$3500
POD Royalty: 70-90% of net
E-book Fee: N/A
E-book Royalty: N/A
goldenpillarpublishing.com
Rating: 7 (fees are high, but include additional services)

Hyperbooks
POD Fee: N/A
POD Royalty: N/A
E-book Fee: $0
E-book Royalty: 90% of retail
hyperbooks.com
Rating: 5 (they don't have an active website)

Infinity
POD Fee: $500
POD Royalty: 20% of retail
E-book Fee: N/A
E-book Royalty: N/A
infinitypublishing.com
Rating: 5 (upfront fees are high)

iUniverse
POD Fee: $450
POD Royalty: 20% of net
E-book Fee: $650
E-book Royalty: 20% of net
iuniverse.com
Rating: 8 (the best of the top three, but high upfront fees with net royalties)

Kingfisher Books
POD Fee: N/A
POD Royalty: N/A
E-book Fee: $0-$90
E-book Royalty: 50-90% of retail
kingfisherbooks.com
Rating: 8 (depends on royalty)

Llumnia Press
POD Fee: $500-$700
POD Royalty: 10-30% of retail
E-book Fee: $200-$700
E-book Royalty: 10-30% of retail
llumnia.com
Rating: 6 (high upfront fees)

London Circle
POD Fee: N/A
POD Royalty: N/A
E-book Fee: $0
E-book Royalty: 35% of retail
londoncircle.com
Rating: 9 (selective,offers good marketing)

Lulu
POD Fee: $.02 per page
POD Royalty: 20% of retail
E-book Fee: Included
E-book Royalty: 20% of retail
lulu.com
Rating: 8 (decent pricing; add-ons still have fees)

Mye-Books
POD Fee: $375-$475
POD Royalty: 30% of retail
E-book Fee: Included
E-book Royalty: 50% of retail
mye-books.com
Rating: 5 (ambiguous language in contract, high upfront fees)

No Spine
POD Fee: N/A
POD Royalty: N/A
E-book Fee: $0
E-book Royalty: 80% of retail
nospine.com
Rating: 8 (good deal if you can drive traffic to your e-book)

Outskirts Press
POD Fee: $200-$1,000
POD Royalty: 25-50% of retail
E-book Fee: $200-$1000
E-book Royalty: 50% of retail
outskirtspress.com
Rating: 3 (high upfront and add-on fees)

Smashwords
POD Fee: N/A
POD Royalty: N/A
E-book Fee: $0
E-Book Royalty: 45-80% of net
smashwords.com
Rating: 4 (high add-on fees, difficult set up and termination)

Stone Dragon Press
POD Fee: $0
POD Royalty: 10% of retail
E-book Fee: N/A
E-book Royalty: N/A
stonedragonpress.com
Rating: 1 (gets exclusive print rights for five years)

Third Millennium
POD Fee: $300
POD Royalty: 90% of retail
E-book Fee: $300
E-book Royalty: 90% of retail
3mpub.com
Rating: 3 (initial fee must be renewed after 2 years)

Trafford
POD Fee: $700-$1400
POD Royalty: 60% of net
E-book Fee: $700-$1400
E-book Royalty: 60% of net
trafford.com
Rating: 3 (high upfront fees, royalties are minimized by net)

U Publish
POD Fee: $400-$500
POD Royalty: 20-40% of retail
E-book Fee: $400-$500
E-book Royalty: 40% of retail
upublish.com
Rating: 5 (high upfront fees)

Virtual Bookworm
POD Fee: $350-$2000
POD Royalty: 50% of net
E-book Fee: $99
E-book Royalty: 50% of net
virtualbookworm.com
Rating: 7 (upfront fees high, but offers free marketing)

Wasteland Press
POD Fee: $200-$1200
POD Royalty: 10-30% of retail
E-book Fee: $75-1200
E-book Royalty: 25% of retail
wastelandpress.com
Rating: 8 (upfront fees high, but includes books)

We-Publish
POD Fee: $575
POD Royalty: 35% of retail
E-book Fee: N/A
E-book Royalty: N/A
we-publish.com
Rating: 8 (high upfront fees)

Wide Thinker
POD Fee: $400
POD Royalty: 10-20% of retail
E-book Fee: $200
E-book Royalty: 50% of retail
widethinker.com
Rating: 3 (they retain rights for three years)

Wild Side Press
POD Fee: $0
POD Royalty: 6-10% of retail
E-book Fee: 0
E-book Royalty: 50% of retail
wildsidepress.com
Rating: 2 (you must sign away your rights for four years)

Writer's Closet
POD Fee: N/A
POD Royalty: N/A
E-book Fee: 0
E-book Royalty: 75% of net
writerscloset.com
Rating: 1 (they retain rights to sell after you terminate contract)

Xlibris
POD Fee: $500-$1600
POD Royalty: 10-25% of retail
E-book Fee: $500-$1600
E-book Royalty: 25-50% of retail
xlibris.com
Rating: 4 (upfront fees and add-ons are very high)

Xulon Press
POD Fee: $1000-$2200
POD Royalty: 30% of net
E-book Fee: N/A
E-book Royalty: N/A
xulonpress.com
Rating: 4 (high fees to place book on alternate websites)

Your Book Publisher
POD Fee: $3.50 per page
POD Royalty: 15% of retail
E-book Fee: N/A
E-book Royalty: N/A
yourbookpublisher.com
Rating: 1 (they retain rights after contract termination)

AMAZON OPTIONS

Straight to Kindle
E-book Fee: $0
E-book Royalty: 30-70% of retail
kdp.amazon.com
Rating: 7 (easy set up, but royalty based on book price)

Create Space
POD Fee: $0
POD Royalty: 60% of net
E-Book Fee: Included
E-book Royalty: 40-60% of net
createspace.com
Rating: 9 (easy set up, decent royalty, add-ons have fees)

www.ingramcontent.com/pod-product-compliance
Lightning Source LLC
Chambersburg PA
CBHW070259300526
45791CB00022B/1659